I0467298

Increasing Collaboration

Published by Createspace LLC
Copyright © 2014 by Adam Collier
Editing by Scott Weaver (chapter 1)
www.scottweaver360.com

First Printing June 2014

Table of Contents

CHAPTER ONE

Engineering Your Collaboration

Useful Models of Collaboration

In corporations, Universities and startup todays collaboration is a must-do skill. No matter how intelligent or experienced we are, a group of collaborating and connected professionals is smarter and faster than the sum of individuals working alone. If we can build relationships and learn to help one another our innovations and careers will accelerate. Organizations will reach goals faster and time spent at work will be more enjoyable. In light of this reality it seems appropriate to analyze collaboration so that we can begin to engineer our collaboration work styles. But, before we discuss collaboration it might be wise to discuss the steps leading to collaboration.

SPECTRUM OF TEAMWORK

There is a spectrum of teamwork and human behavior from collaboration to competition, see figure below. On the competition end of the spectrum trust is non-existent and every tool of competition is on the table. On the other end of the spectrum is collaboration in which ideas and credit are shared and cooperative open teaching is common.

The remainder of this book covers the collaboration side of the spectrum and assumes that open competition is not a major problem in your organization. However, If open competition is a major problem its solution is the same for increasing collaboration, that us working on trust and we will cover the trust issue later in this book.

Collaboration is the most effective and efficient way to learn, to invent, to provide value, to tap the ingenuity of employees and to grow your career. *"There's only one thing that all the successful companies in the world have in common: None was started by one person."* — Ernesto Sirolli

Miriam Webster's definition of collaboration: col·lab·o·rate **verb** \kə-ˈla-bə-ˌrāt\: to work with another person or group in order to achieve or do something. We must work with one another based on proximity many times however it is not a given that we can effectively work with one another in relationship. Human relationship can be a toxic, a distant or a vibrant relationship filled with helpful interactions and benevolent give and take behaviors. Not only is this a reality we face it is has become the key to organizational productivity. How we work together determines the speed of our organization, it determines the effectiveness and relevance of our teams.

The majority of my research on this topic focused either on the tools and i.e. the statistics of collaboration and productivity, or on the people side, how to work with other people from diverse backgrounds. It would seem that most people just assume if you have a diverse team that collaboration will automatically be robust and healthy.

Collaboration content nowadays there seems to be the mandatory diversity is better mantra that we gained two decades ago. I have been a member of very diverse teams, teams that were ethnic and gender melting pots that were resistant to collaboration, some of these teams would work on the same things in parallel and would openly compete and undermine one another. I've experienced this within teams and separate teams competing to win, behave in ways opposite to collaboration. Diversity helps but in and of itself diversity does not necessarily result in true collaboration or more effective teams. There is something deeper to look at in understanding team productivity and collaboration and with this book I want to go deeper.

You would like a model that covers the "what's in it for me?" and "feel good for doing a good job" problem that every team, and almost every individual struggles with as you grow a career.

Every professional can understand and engineer their collaboration relationships based on a four ring trust model. In my experience I want a model that addresses the proverbial 'elephant in the room' which is trust. There are certain people that we encounter in our careers that are not worthy of our trust. To build a working team and to ignore the concept of trust, and for leaders to expect people to collaborate with untrustworthy peers because they say so or because it is good for business I believe is a recipe for half-hearted collaboration at best. At worst it is a recipe to lose quality team members.

For example, there have been times that I've been asked to work with colleagues that was very uncomfortable for me. They had proven themselves untrustworthy to me on several occasions. There was no a mutual respect and good-will present between us. If you've spent any time in corporate America you might understand

Not to go into too many details, the bottom-line was that I just did not trust them with my insights, my knowledge and my collaboration. They may have been great employees, intelligent and creative but, given the choice I won't work with them. This should be ok, we should be able to say at a reasonable level, all politeness aside, 'I can't work with that person' or 'please don't make me collaborate with that person' out loud to leadership.

A healthy organization will have managers that allow freedom and will be prosperous enough to allow team members freedom to avoid certain people. Essentially allowing this freedom is leadership acknowledging and giving room for trust to openly influence a team culture.

In light of this important trust issue I want to introduce a concept that helps explain personal collaboration which takes into account degrees of trust.

The way that most people already collaborate and do teamwork professionally can be explained with what I call a **rings of collaboration** model. Like the rings around Saturn, the rings of collaboration have closer and further orbits depending on the person and trust level.

Senior leadership within most companies trains employees along this model. We use rings of trust naturally, in fact some collaboration outside the circles of trust can get a person fired, fined or even thrown into prison. For example, sharing manufacturing secrets with an industrial spy from China.   Trust issues between employees should be talked about more, to assume that all employees will trust one another and collaborate freely for the sake of company is not realistic.

As trust is openly discussed perhaps the unprofessional and unfair aspects, the very reasons that we mistrust within some of our team cultures will begin to be less dominant.

RINGS OF COLLABORATION

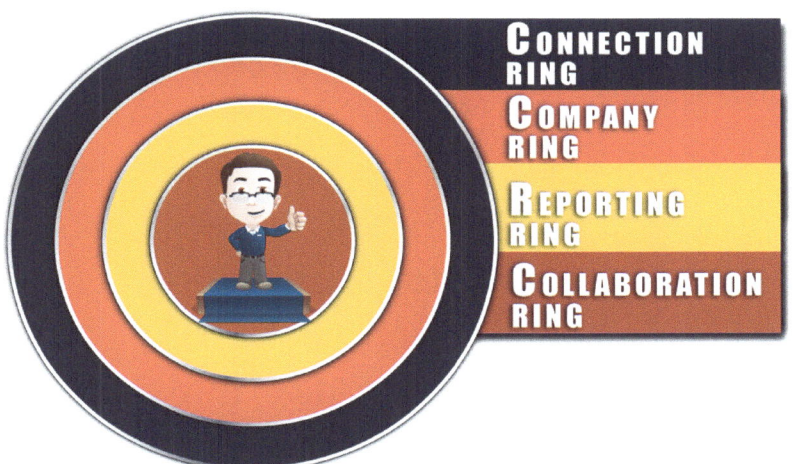

CONNECTION RING

COMPANY RING

REPORTING RING

COLLABORATION RING

To best explain these rings of collaboration imagine a scientist who is working on process improvement that will save her company manufacturing time and investment.

As is the case with every complex task particularly with processes or technology innovation collaboration with other people is necessary for timely and accurate decisions.

This scientist's outer ring of collaboration, the **Connection Ring,** is one in which she simply reports to the outside world what she is working on, this relationship is at arms length. She makes broad and vague statements, 'I work in the ABC division I am (*this type of scientist*).'

This connection ring hears not much more than her elevator speech. Trust is low, formality is high and secrets are not revealed. **The Company Ring**, moving closer to the professional is one in which she has conversations internal to the company; she makes more detailed descriptions of what her project is doing. She may share the reason for the project; she may share who her leadership team is and her supporting team.

She may even share high level strategy. In this ring only company-internal details are allowed but the inner details are not shared as they are on a need to know basis only.

The third-ring, **Reporting Ring,** mostly involves her direct leadership; this is often where real teaching begins. Periodically she reports to this layer in detail, sharing mostly the technical progress and future plans.

She may teach her leadership or her students what she understands in detail but only after she understands the concepts and has learned them from a public source or learned them herself on the job through experimentation or experience. This ring of manager or students does not help to guide experimentation to any significant degree; suggestions are only taken into consideration.

This layer also includes interested peers, and fellow professionals who may be interested, but not necessarily involved to the same level as direct collaborators. Internal reports can be shared with this layer but only after the content is well packaged, mostly understood and these reports are intended to impress and to educate management or to teach students.

The fourth ring, **Collaboration Ring**, is composed of fellow team members, professionals, scientists, engineers or technicians who routinely help to learn; to study and to experiment on the project. These team members directly discuss the nuts and bolts of the project and directly contribute to the progress of the project.

Inventions and credits are shared in this layer (ideally); this is the closest layer and may or may not include formal leadership..

There may be a senior person guiding the progress technically but management level leadership is not necessary depending on the leadership culture of the organization.

How easily professionals, that is "you, the reader" allow peers into your collaboration ring is one indicator of your organization's overall health. The ease at which you allow people into your collaboration ring can also be a major factor of the speed at which you and your organization can innovate. Professionals who are able to work more within that collaboration ring, who are able to navigate culture to build trust even with the most difficult to work with peers typically do better in career growth than do those who are not able. Every professional should begin to allow the right people into their collaboration ring by first eliminating five trust-destroying behaviors. I've seen (and done) several but the following five are common, if you've seen or are yourself engaging in these behaviors then try to stop them but also start calling them out when you see them in yourself and in others   The first trust destroying behavior that I've seen is *unfair litmus tests* based on identity politics that only a few can pass. The litmus test may be degree level attained, it may be based on quality of University attended, within the university setting it may be even grades or advisor quality. The litmus test may be based on even political or religious beliefs, it may be based on friendships only.

A second trust destroying behavior that needs to be called out is *promotion of incompetent leadership.* Incompetent leadership can even dissuade collaboration, sometimes even intentionally. Now, when I say 'incompetent' I don't mean that the new leader is incompetent, they may be technically brilliant but that they may be incompetent in the dynamics of leadership and how their behavior now affects culture and people.

They may not understand team dynamics and still function as a competitive individual contributor and do damage to team-work.

A third trust destroying behavior is *manager-only collaboration*. This is likely due to a competitive (and therefore insecure) culture. Only the managers and their direct reports seem to collaborate this may be a sign that the culture is very untrusting and the collaboration that is occurring is out of necessity only. Manager-only collaboration is at a shallow level because peers are busy competing.

A fourth trust destroying behavior is faux collaboration, this is a passive aggressive collaboration attitude that essentially says: 'I'll teach you what I am doing, but don't try to control things', this is collaboration in form only, pretending to take recommendations in order to portray collaboration.

The fifth trust-damaging behavior that I've seen in a variety of different types of organizations is what I call *idea theft*

Idea theft occurs when new ideas are automatically rejected when presented by lower level employees to leadership or senior team members. Later, these same ideas conveniently reappear by the more senior team members when no one is paying attention. Credit for the great suggestion is then not shared with the lower level employees. This behavior creates a strong resistance to collaboration. If this is common then there is a lack of trust perpetuating the culture and an unhealthy competitive tone dominates and reproduces itself within teams. Senior management is in the best position to intervene and stop this behavior.

A major factor in the level of collaboration is the personality of the leader, is he an open person? Is she trusting of others? Are they young and ambitious with a need to get a lot of credit to grow in their career? Are they arrogant and only will accept direct collaboration from certain people who have passed their tests?

Healthy and productive collaboration occurs when professionals learn to trust based on professional reasons not based on systems of friendships or prejudices. **Successful people are able to use the trust ring model to understand their team culture, to locate their own trust levels and to boost their careers and team effectiveness through increased collaboration.** Direct collaboration with fellow employees where knowledge is shared freely is financially and emotionally valuable to the careers and to our teams. The easier it is for you to get yourself and your team members to work within the direct collaboration ring the healthier and faster your organization will function. This trust ring model of collaboration I think accurately depicts the state of collaboration amongst professionals. This model can also be used to engineer our collaboration work styles which is so critical to careers and team effectiveness.

CHAPTER TWO

Breaking Down Barriers to Collaboration - for the individual

Careers are better off with more people in the collaboration ring, especially the right people. When we naively allow in people that cannot be trusted, for whatever reason, we are harmed. However the right people can boost a career and even entire organizations in amazing ways . **Every person can break down the barriers to collaboration and increase the number of trust-worthy people in their direct collaboration layer by following these four steps.**

Step 1 is to accept that collaboration relationships must be **mutual**. For collaboration to really impact a career we must buy-in to the idea that collaboration is valuable to us personally and to the organization as a whole. The answer to the 'what's in it for me?' question must be something worthwhile and if it is not, then why bother to grow our collaboration?

We wont go all the way, we will approach collaboration in a selfish manner, and therefore it will not work for us. The correct answer to the 'what's in it for me?' question is two-fold.

Collaboration is good for our careers because we benefit from the knowledge, the experiences and the wisdom of peers, it speeds up our learning curves considerably. Secondly, collaboration is about mutual benefit, good-will for yourself and for the organization, there is shared destiny. Realize that a successful organization, a successful team and successful peers will benefit you personally in the long run.

Step 2 is to **identify who is currently in your reporting and collaboration rings**, what are their personalities?, why do you trust them?, are they useful to you professionally or is it simply a friendship, is it a one-way relationship? Have they actually been a detriment to your career but you are oblivious to this?

In a private location list these people, sketch out your own rings of collaboration. Profiling these people will give you insight into your collaboration style and may help you to identify new collaboration candidates. This can also help you to think about moving in or moving out people in each of these rings. Upon doing this you may realize that no one is in your direct collaboration layer. This may be the case for a variety of reasons, perhaps you have a hard time trusting, and/or perhaps you have behaved in ways in the past that few trust you.

Perhaps the culture in your organization is so toxic that trust and mutual good-will is almost non-existent. If this is the case then don't panic you can still build a collaboration ring, it may be difficult, depending on your situation but it can be done with intentionality.

"Trust is a rare and valuable resource in the marketplace" - John Gerzema

Step 3 is to **identify one or two new candidates for your direct collaboration ring**, these may be people who you admire and think you can trust. They may be people who are below you or above you in seniority or rank, they may be people who have knowledge that you need or someone you simply want to learn from. They may be members of a team or department that you are working with currently. This step is intended to help you to begin to engineer your collaboration relationships.

To consider new people for your collaboration ring, reach out and see if you can trust them with direct collaboration. You can do this by asking them to do something for you, by sharing information with them, or by asking trusted friends their opinion. Trying all three is a great option.

I have tested people by sharing information, I share with them a little about what I know or what I've observed in experimentation. Then I simply watch how they respond.

Being generous first is a great way to test people. I have done this on several occasions, some people will take the information and reciprocate nothing, they use it to their personal advantage and I don't hear back from them. In response to this I could only assume 1) they don't want to collaborate with me and/or 2) they are not trustworthy with my insight. Either way they fail the mutual good will or the trust test. I have done this with different people on other occasions and they show appreciation for the insight, they reciprocate the sharing of their information, they propose experiments or learning's together and even ask for help on parts of their project.

It is not difficult to test people and to quickly learn who to trust with the your direct collaboration ring.

Step 4 is to relax and start collaborating, enjoy the give and take of a mutual and trusted collaboration network. Long-term these increases in real collaboration will help careers and organizational performance.

I have laid out four steps to help individuals increase the amount of collaboration in their day to day. Few dispute the fact that we need one another to create and to produce more and to do so faster. Collaboration is the best tool for increasing productivity and speed of innovation, implement these steps and watch your career accelerate. The next chapter is designed for the leader to help her or him to increase the amount of collaboration within the organization they lead.

CHAPTER THREE

Breaking Down Barriers to Collaboration, for the leader.

"Trust ultimately is a business driver and enabler of transformation and positive change." - Cynthia Figge, CSRHub

There are several ways this information can help you, if you are a leader you should strive to get as many of your people as possible working in their direct collaboration ring. If they work in this level of interaction then your organization will be faster, more innovative and overall employee satisfaction will be higher. You as a leader have more power over these collaboration layers than you might think, you are not simply an impartial observer of what is; you can impact the collaboration level within your teams. You have power to change this because you have the most power over your culture, you can create trust as a value in your culture, it is not necessarily easy but it is possible and it may be easier than you think.

Based on my experience in working in and in leading teams more than 90% of team problems are relationship based.

Every leader can cause their team members to grow their collaboration layer by using the following five collaboration-enabling activities.

The first collaboration enabling activity is to **share your vision about collaboration** in the next vision-casting speech, meeting and one-on-one. In these meetings acknowledge the need for trust and ask your people what would it take to get us collaborating at a higher level. This may expose some of the hindrances to collaboration within your team.

Some teams are thrown together by projects by necessity. For example, a project leader from TX is suddenly leading a project with ten engineers from NY, three scientists from Germany, four engineers from southeast Asia and three commercial leaders from MA. They don't know one another, barely understand one another culturally and all communication is formal and distant.

How can the leader get the level of collaboration that is required which is so critical to project success? By virtue of necessity these professionals have been thrown into their third ring, the reporting layer. I would argue that after everyone understands the project goals and roles of team members that the leader openly discuss the *elephant in the room*, which is trust. Gently work on relationships, verbalize the need for trust, verbalize the need for open and direct collaboration not with a heavy-handed "do it my way" approach but with an gentle and open appeal.

Undoubtedly some of these team members will not be trustworthy people. There may be underlying prejudices, stereotypes and just plain lack of good-will. However the good thing is they are all in one another's reporting ring of collaboration by

"The first dysfunction of a team is the absence of trust" – Patrick Lencioni

default, the leader should take advantage of that, take turns involving everyone, push for connections, push for travel to connect everyone if in the budget.

Sometimes personal information and cultural differences can be shared to break down formality. It will not take long to identify the trustworthy team members and collaboration ring relationships will naturally form. If they do, highlight those relationships as an example, discuss trust, collaboration and mutual benefit openly in meetings and one-on-one. The leader sets the tone of the team in powerful ways. Expect trust issues, expect getting credit issues, expect to hear some resentment, expect to hear these things, don't be surprised by them and have a plan ready to fix them.

The second collaboration enabling activity for leaders is to consider **starting a blog**, there are few better tools to cast vision, to share your plans and to connect with your team these days than a weekly or monthly leaders blog. You can set up a private in-company blog with the help of IT or an external blog using Wordpress, if you want help with this reach out to me and I will point you in the right direction . If you don't like to write, you could speak out your blog posts and have an assistant annotate. There are even services out there where you call in to a voicemail inbox with a spoken "blog post", they transcribe your words and send it back to you in email. View blogging as a powerful means of communication or as another means to build healthy culture. If you are reluctant to do this, consider it anyway, as a service to those you lead.

The third collaboration enabling activity is to work to **build trust in your team/ organization**, of course this is a long-term activity. If there are years of culture with low trust this will take a while to repair. In general, trust starts at the top, create a clear and well defined vision and purpose for the organization, make sure your leadership team understands and buy's into this purpose and vision.

Have an off-site picnic or retreat, one where new relationships can be built. You want friendships to flourish, work to create this. Communicate this vision often to the overall organization; communicate it so much that it feels like you are over-communicating. A clear vision with united leaders will go a long way to increasing trust within your organization.

The fourth collaboration-enabling activity for a leader is to work to repair trust in short bursts.

This is done primarily by **acknowledging failures of trust** in the culture, if the culture is notorious for being unfair or has a few super-heroes then acknowledge that failure. Ask for more trust between people, ask for anonymous reasons that people do not trust, submitted directly to you. Ask your employees to forgive leadership and to forgive one another.

The fifth collaboration enabling activity is to **ask your people to teach**. Most people, be they introverted or extroverted love to share what they know, especially knowledge workers. Teaching is a powerful tool to get people to open up. One great display of this can be seen during a poster session.

A poster session can be a culture engineering tool for a leader if it is done properly. Nothing stimulates collaboration like a poster session. In a poster session, typically secretive and self serving employees suddenly are intentionally teaching and putting their work on display, their knowledge and their future plans. It is usually a 180 degree turn from their typical guarded untrusting behavior. This happens simply because they were asked to teach; to some people a poster session is almost like a competition of who can teach or who can prepare the best poster. The next time you are at a poster session take a step back and notice all of the collaboration.

Bonus: Another tool to increasing collaboration is what I call **supervised collaboration**. If there are experts that your people can and should be collaborating with somewhere outside of your department or division try reaching out to his or her manager and ask for collaboration. Set up this collaboration relationship through leadership. When people realize that their leaders are watching how they collaborate and interact with one another there is a greater probability of fruitful collaborations.

CHAPTER FOUR

Conclusion and Calls To Action

In summary, we collaborate according to four levels in concentric rings, based on trust. The outer ring we call the connection ring and includes acquaintances outside of our companies, the people to whom we give elevator speeches. The second ring is the company ring, these are acquaintances inside our company or organization, people we barely know yet share organization level secrets with by virtue of the fact that they are fellow team members. The third ring is the reporting ring, this is the layer that we report our results to yet do not collaborate easily with for lack of trust or need to retain credit. The inner and closest ring is the collaboration ring, these are the people that we trust with daily experiments, data and share credit with readily.

Every person can break down barriers to collaboration and increase the number of trust worthy people in their collaboration layer by following these four steps

1) Accept the fact that collaboration is valuable to your career and that it must be a mutual give and take relationship. 2) Identify and profile who is currently in your collaboration ring (if anyone). This will give you insight into your ability to trust and if they are really helping you 3) Identify two new candidates for collaboration, this begins your collaboration overhaul and helps you to start to be intentional about collaboration and teach you how to identify people you can and can not trust.   4) Relax and start collaborating, enjoy the give and take. If you mess up and realize you chose wrong it is okay, this process can be repeated throughout your career as people and projects come and go.

Every leader can cause their employees to work more within their collaboration ring by using the following five collaboration-enabling activities.

"...greater than 90% of team problems are relationship based."

First, share you collaboration vision with your team members. Second, seriously consider starting your own leadership blog. This can be a public blog or one specifically designed for your organization. Third is to begin to strive for a culture of trust in your organization. This is a long-term activity but is it important as a leader to have the mindset of trust building. The fourth collaboration-enabling activity is to repair trust by acknowledging trust failures and by asking for forgiveness for past failures in trust. And finally the fifth collaboration-enabling activity is to ask your people to teach one another. Few things stimulate collaboration like asking your people to teach management and one another what they know through a poster session or a series of reporting presentations.

Final call to action, as you can see every step or activity in both the individual and leadership chapters is itself a call to action. However, there is one more thing that I want to ask you to do. I would ask you to not get discouraged, managing human relationships can be difficult, it may take years to impact your collaboration ring or the collaboration ring of your teams, just don't get discouraged or give up working at collaboration it is worth your time and effort.

About the Author:

Adam K. Collier has worked in early stage technology R&D for the past 17 years, he earned his Bachelors in Material Science and Engineering degree from Alfred University. Adam and his wife Melanie like to spend time with their five young children. Adam blogs about human creativity, innovation and science at collieradam.com

www.ingramcontent.com/pod-product-compliance
Lightning Source LLC
Chambersburg PA
CBHW041141180526
45159CB00002BB/698